the happiest hour

DELICIOUS MOCKTAILS FOR A FABULOUS MOMS' NIGHT IN

Debbie Podlogar

creator of Mocktail Mom™

ROCK
POINT

Contents

Not Past Our Prime

Spicy Momma Mocktails

Hot Flash Mommas Need Frozen Drinks

Buzzworthy Brunch Minus the Buzz

Mint to Be Mocktails

Mules for Days

Sharing Is Caring

Holidays without Hangovers

Introduction

Back before I accidentally became sober, the only mocktail I could have named was a Shirley Temple. If you're a mom—of a human, a pet, or just in spirit—and you want to move away from mommy wine culture and start living an alcohol-free (or reduced) lifestyle, I'm here to help you have fun drinking while you're *not* drinking!

Like many, I grew up with the idea that you were either a normal drinker or you had a "problem." For thirty-plus years, I didn't need nor rely on alcohol—I wasn't born with a bottle of Chardonnay in hand. It wasn't until I went through some really hard times that I started to look at wine as a companion and friend. After nine years of emotional turmoil (consisting of my daughter's recovery from a critical illness, my divorce, a battle with breast cancer, and the loss of my parents), I found I was using wine to numb the pain. Slowly, I became a "Wine Mom." Whichever wine is your companion, you know it's a habit when you pour that first glass while cooking, then enjoy another (or two) during dinner, and continue all the way up until bedtime (or until you pass out on the couch!). A glass of wine was a reward at the end of a work day, to relax and "take the edge off," but I was also checked out mentally and emotionally on myself and my loved ones. And I didn't like the person I had become.

As I approached my fiftieth birthday, I found myself waking up most days with a mommy wine headache (a.k.a. hangover) and I was at an all-time low of shame and despair. I knew I did not want the next decade of my life to look like the last. So, on December 31, 2020, I challenged myself to do a dry month and bought my first bottle of nonalcoholic wine. It was one of the hardest days of my life and at the time, nothing seemed more pointless than wine without alcohol. But one of the saddest parts, for me, was the fear of telling the people I was closest to. The idea of anyone thinking I had a "problem" kept me from speaking about it. Thankfully, I was lucky enough to find a safe and supportive community of like-minded women who were also sober-curious. They too were evaluating their relationship with alcohol, and I quickly learned that I was not the only one struggling!

Once I removed alcohol from my life, I began to thrive in a way I hadn't in a long time. I started to feel like *me* again. My life turned in an entirely new direction as I began experimenting with mocktails and sharing my recipes and milestones on social media. I have since experienced so many benefits of living alcohol-free (for over 1,000 days!) and I want to be an encouragement to all of you! You will never regret a night of mocktails, I can promise you that. Whether you are sober curious or dry, *the fun is not over*! There are so many options and I'm certain you'll find some favorites in this recipe book.

Big Time Cheers from the great state of Kentucky and lots of love!

Shopping for Mocktails

There has been an explosion of nonalcoholic options across the globe, and with so many on offer, deciding what to purchase can feel overwhelming. Before we get into what you should buy to successfully become a mocktail mom, I want to prepare you for what to expect when shopping.

Unfortunately, most big box and liquor stores place the alcohol-free section all the way in the back, or right next to their alcoholic counterparts. The first few times I went shopping, I had to put my blinders on and walk right on past my old lovers (the Joshes and Kim Crawfords; maybe you know the crew?). If you're not ready for that, there are plenty of online stores that have the essentials. For beginners, I recommend starting with one or two bottles of a nonalcoholic spirit, an alcohol-free wine, or some cans of nonalcoholic beer.

Try new things! Be open to discovering new alternatives for your old favorites, but do not feel like you need to buy everything on the shelf. Take your time experimenting and have fun with it! You never know, you might find the new love of your life in the nonalcoholic section!

Spirit Alternatives

Spirit alternatives were crafted to provide an elevated drinking experience without the side effects of alcohol. In recent years, the demand for nonalcoholic alternatives has skyrocketed and we are seeing many brands producing a "zero" alcohol version to their traditional counterparts.

According to the FDA, less than 0.5% ABV is considered nonalcoholic. Labels may also say "nonalcoholic" or "dealcoholized," which means the alcohol has been removed, but there may still be a trace left—just not enough to get you drunk or buzzed. Many of the things I drink are nonalcoholic or dealcoholized, and I am comfortable enjoying these while maintaining a nonalcoholic lifestyle. Always drink what you feel comfortable with and *read* the labels.

If you are looking for zero-proof options, there are such things! Zero-proof wines are most likely crafted with botanicals like juniper, coriander, hibiscus, lavender, clove, or ginger. The same goes for zero-proof spirits. For those who wish to only drink 0.0% ABV, there are options for you!

If you're completely new to nonalcoholic drinks, I recommend joining my Facebook group called **Mocktails & Non-Alcoholic Drinks | Big Time Cheers with Mocktail Mom**, where you can connect with others in an alcohol-free/sober-curious space and get plenty of tips and tricks. Just remember, all of us have different taste buds, and amazingly, your tastes will change the longer you go without consuming alcohol!

Your Alcohol-Free Home Setup

You don't need to be a bartender or a mixologist to start making mocktails. I'm certainly not! Once you jump into the world of mocktails, you will discover so many amazing things to drink. Mocktails don't have to be complicated, but many are much more sophisticated than the wine I used to drink from screw-top bottles. They can be beautifully garnished or simply prepared in a mason jar. It's up to you how fancy you want your mocktails to be, what's most important is to have *fun* making them and *enjoy* drinking them!

Your alcohol-free home setup can be as simple as creating a mocktail station or a full mocktail bar, depending on how you want to incorporate mocktails into your lifestyle. Starting with only a mocktail station and jumping into the world of nonalcoholic drinks helped me be 100 percent successful on my alcohol-free journey. From there, I leveled up to a full at-home mocktail bar, which quickly expanded from the cocktail shaker I had to search for in the back of my kitchen cabinet, dust off, and figure out how to use, to my husband bringing home two beverage refrigerators to help store and stock my expansive collection of nonalcoholic drinks and spirits.

Here, I offer suggestions based on my own experience creating an alcohol-free space, but there's no right or wrong way to get started on your mocktail journey, just take it one step at a time. It's a journey, not a race!

The Mocktail Station

To make a mocktail station, place a special tray or charger plate on your kitchen counter to help surf the urge and avoid temptation during the witching hour of meal prep. Your mocktail station doesn't have to be filled with many items. The most important are a cocktail shaker, a muddler, a nonalcoholic spirit of choice, a fizz (mixer) of choice (like ginger beer, tonic, or sparkling water), some citrus, your favorite glass, and a recipe book. These items will have you prepared to make simple starter mocktails and give you a foundation to build upon.

The Mocktail Bar

As I mentioned earlier, for the mocktails you choose to make, your alcohol-free home bar can be as simple or fancy as you like. So, let's start with stocking the basics.

Tools

If you don't have the exact tool or equipment, don't let that hold you back from your mocktail adventures. Substitutions and improvisations are welcome pathways to mixing and experimenting with your drinks.

Bar spoon: Used for stirring drinks when shaking isn't required, as it's long enough to reach the bottom of the mixing glass without making a mess. If you don't have a bar spoon, use a long iced-tea spoon. This is one of those tools I didn't think I needed, but I do in fact use it regularly.

Blender: A high-powered blender is great for creating delicious frozen mocktails.

Channel knife: A channel knife is perfect for cutting fruit peels into thin twists, which can then be used to express over a drink, rub along the rim, or add as a garnish.

Citrus squeezer: A much-needed tool for adding fresh-squeezed juice to your mocktails, therefore elevating the flavor. I didn't have one at the beginning of my mocktail journey; I used bottled juice and still do when I don't have fresh citrus. Surprisingly, the citrus squeezer is fun to use and another opportunity to take out life's frustrations during your mocktail making.

Cocktail shaker: The two most popular types are a cobbler shaker and a Boston shaker. A cobbler shaker has three pieces and is the easiest for mixing, shaking, and pouring drinks, with a built-in strainer that keeps the ice from pouring out. Most professional bartenders use a Boston shaker, which consists of two parts: typically two metal containers, or one metal container and one glass container. I have not completely mastered the art of the Boston shaker. I can't make a seal nor break the seal to properly pour the drink through a separate strainer. All I make is a mess, not a mocktail. If you don't have a cocktail shaker, use a mason jar or protein shaker cup.

Cutting board and small knife: You probably already have these, but they are worth mentioning. You will want a small cutting board and a sharp knife for cutting fruit and garnishes.

Extra refrigerator: This may sound "extra," but if you have the space, having a refrigerator just to store your nonalcoholic options is a big-time bonus. Especially if you live with others who still drink, you will appreciate having a secure space to reach for a beverage. I'd suggest buying a used fridge for your garage or a beverage refrigerator for your house.

Frother: This little handheld device is fun to use to whip up toppings for drinks and froth milk and creamy ingredients used in mocktails or coffee drinks.

Ice molds: I love ice and almost always fill my entire glass full. My collection includes large round molds and molds in a variety of shapes and interesting forms. I sometimes add fruit, herbs, flowers, and other edible things to elevate my ice game. When a drink calls for crushed ice, and you don't have a freezer that makes it, just place ice cubes in a resealable plastic bag, place a towel over the bag, and smash it with a rolling pin or a meat tenderizer.

Jigger: Am I the only one that heard this word and immediately thought it was some kind of Irish step dance? Well, it's actually a measuring tool with measurements printed in the tiniest font. The professionals use jiggers, but all you need is something that can measure at least ½ to 2 ounces (15 to 60 ml). I prefer mini angled measuring cups that I found online and don't require me to dig out a pair of reading glasses. Hello, over fifty and fabulous!

Mixing glass: A mixing glass is typically a thick and durable glass with a heavier base, a wide mouth, and a spout for a smooth pour. It allows blending and chilling in one container, as well as stirring the ingredients with a bar spoon rather than shaking.

Muddler: A muddler is used to smash fruit or gently release a fresh herb's oil and aroma. I sometimes take out all my aggression when I muddle fruit—smashing fruit is cheaper than therapy! Be careful not to over-muddle herbs, such as mint, because it can make the drink taste bitter. Find a basic flat-bottomed stainless-steel muddler. If you don't have a muddler, try using the end of a wooden spoon.

Stainless-steel straws: I'm a huge fan of stainless-steel straws. They're more sustainable and they elevate your straw-drinking experience, IMHO.

Strainers: There are three types of strainers I like to use: fine-mesh, Julep, and Hawthorne. A fine-mesh strainer is useful for removing pulp or small ingredient particles from drinks that call for "double straining." This ensures a smooth mocktail without unintended bits floating in it (and maybe making their way to your teeth—nothing says "delicious mocktails" more than a bit of mint stuck in between your front teeth). I use the Julep when a recipe calls for a mixing glass, because it allows you to pour the drink without the ice and larger ingredients falling in. The Hawthorne does the same thing but is more commonly used for drinks poured from the tin or glass of a Boston shaker.

Nonalcoholic Recommendations

The best way to switch from cocktails to mocktails is to swap your favorite alcoholic beverages for their nonalcoholic counterparts. Stick with what you know and let your tastes and favorites naturally expand.

Beers: If you were a beer drinker, you will be pleasantly surprised by the expansive varieties still available to you—from stouts to IPAs to seasonal crafts. Have a few cans on hand to make shandies or micheladas, or to enjoy on their own while watching a game. Big Time Cheers to NA beers and watching sports!

Bitters: Some people are comfortable using traditional bitters in their mocktails, but there are nonalcoholic bitters too. Think of bitters as the salt and pepper of the recipe, like liquid flavoring that changes and enhances the profile of your drink. A brand I love is All The Bitter, made entirely without alcohol and crafted by a wonderful husband-and-wife team who were once sommeliers of the 3-star Michelin restaurant The French Laundry in California.

Spirits: If you're just getting started, choose nonalcoholic spirits that are a one-to-one substitute for their alcoholic counterpart, such as rum, tequila, whiskey, and gin. Know that many have a recommended six month storage life and are not meant to be enjoyed neat or straight, which means they're perfect for mocktails!

Wines: There are two main types of nonalcoholic wine: ones where the alcohol has been removed, and ones made with ingredients such as kombucha, tea, or vinegar. Enjoy in a simple sangria or mimosa, or on its own. Dealcoholized wines are one of my favorite things to drink in the evening, despite mocktails having a special place in my heart.

Glassware

I had no idea how much glassware played a role in what I was drinking. At the start of my alcohol-free journey, I had a scare one morning when I found my "BEST MOM EVER" wine tumbler on my bedside table. Immediately, I had a flashback to pre-sober me and thought, "Oh no! I did it again! I drank again." The disappointment in myself was staggering. However, after fully waking up, I realized it was only leftover nonalcoholic wine. That experience made it click that while I had changed my drinking habits, there was no other representation of that change in my life. That tumbler was a symbol of my past mommy-wine-culture drinking days and I needed a clean slate. In other words, new glassware.

I recommend shopping at second-hand stores for glassware, so you don't have to buy an entire set (unless you want to!). Toss out anything that holds the lingering reminder of your drinking days and find some fun, festive, or fancy glassware that suits your new lifestyle! Use the following as a reference for new glassware.

 Beer mug: This is basically a large sturdy glass. Put it in the freezer before pouring your beer, for those of you that like your beer cold.

 Champagne flute: A flute is perfect for your nonalcoholic sparkling wines and champagne mocktails.

Coupe glass: A thin-stemmed glass with a wide bowl at the top is made for martinis to daiquiris or any drink that needs to be shaken or stirred and doesn't call for ice cubes.

 Irish coffee glass: As in the name, this is the ideal glass for preparing Irish coffees, which is a combination of nonalcoholic whiskey and coffee.

 Margarita glass: There are so many options for a marg like a classic wide rim margarita glass or a stemless glass.

 Martini glass: Different from the coupe glass, it has a V-shaped bowl and is great for not only serving martinis but also cosmos.

 Mason jar: One of my personal favorites—they're just so dang easy! Find them with or without a handle, or with a screw-top lid, and make almost any mocktail in them.

 Moscow mule copper mug: The signature and namesake copper mug insulates the temperature of chilled ginger beer, keeping the mocktail cooler longer.

 Rocks glass: A short glass with a sturdy base meant to serve drinks made mostly with spirits. There are only a few nonalcoholic spirits that can be enjoyed on the rocks, but feel free to use it for any of your mocktails.

Pantry Staples

Now that we've covered what you can add to your home mocktail bar, there are some staple ingredients you should keep in your pantry and refrigerator, as they are multifunctional for everyday drinks and food.

Apple cider vinegar: I discovered that adding a bit of ACV to mocktail recipes brings back that same *bite* of a crisp chardonnay.

Coconut water: Coconut water brings an extra layer of hydration to any mocktail. Not only is it good for you, it also adds a hint of tropical flavor.

Egg white: Some recipes call for raw egg whites. I know, it sounded crazy to me too! But it works! However, if you are pregnant or vegan and need an alternative, try using aquafaba, or the juice from a can of chickpeas.

Ginger beer: Some ginger beers have alcohol, but many do not. The brands I love are Q's and Reed's, with the latter supplying a zero-sugar option as well!

Herbs (fresh and seasonal): Adding fresh herbs enhances your drink's appearance, aroma, and flavor. I like to keep mint, basil, rosemary, and lavender on hand. (Pro tip: Make herbs last with herbal ice cubes. Simply add the herbs to the tray, fill with water, and freeze.)

Jalapeños: Whenever I want a bit of spice added to my drinks, I always have on hand a jar of jalapeños, as I also use the brine from the jar for some of my drinks.

Lemon and lime juice: Many mocktail recipes call for lemon or lime juice, as the sour, acidic profile adds a freshness that brightens the flavor of a drink. To skip the measuring, half a lime is about equal to ½ ounce lime juice. However, if you're short on time and availability, the bottled option works just fine!

Sparkling water: I love my mocktails with extra fizz, or as the professionals call it, *effervescence*. Adding sparkling water enriches the overall mouthfeel and helps to balance the flavor. My top brand recommendations are Liquid Death, Spindrift, and Topo Chico. You can also make your own sparkling water (and save money and packaging) with a SodaStream.

Sweeteners: Sugar can be an issue for mocktails, so try to use sweeteners that don't increase the sugar content of your drink. For granulated sugar, I like the brand Swerve. For every mention of simple syrup in this book, I used the monk fruit–based simple syrup brand, Swoon because they have no sugar. You can also use agave nectar, honey, or the mixer Zevi.

Tajín seasoning or chili lime salt: If you want to level up the kick of your mocktail, add some Tajín seasoning or chili lime salt to the rim of your glass to ensure that each sip has the spice you're craving.

Just
Getting
Started

Do It for You

Margarita on the Rocks

Whip up homemade margaritas straight from your alcohol-free home bar! There is nothing fancy here, but your friends will surely be impressed. This recipe is just a standard margarita, but go wild and add some fun flavors if you want. The possibilities are endless.

Ice cubes

2 ounces NA tequila

1 ounce lime juice

½ ounce orange juice

½ ounce agave nectar

Lime wedges, for the rim and garnishing

Tajín seasoning or salt, for the rim

To a cocktail shaker with some ice, add the NA tequila, lime and orange juices, and agave. Shake until chilled.

If desired, prepare your glass of choice by rubbing the rim with the flesh of a lime wedge, then dip the rim in a plate of Tajín seasoning—or salt if you don't like it spicy.

Strain the drink into the prepared glass with some fresh ice cubes.

Garnish with the remaining lime wedge.

Wind Beneath My Wings

Cosmopolitan

My mom wasn't much of a drinker, but she did love herself a Cosmo . . . or two. Once, when my mom, my older sister, Rachel, and I were in NYC to see Kristin Chenoweth on Broadway, we stopped at the Marriott Times Square bar beforehand. Mom had one Cosmo and we almost had to carry her to the theater. We had the best time giggling through Times Square on the way to the show. For this drink, NA vodkas are a little harder to find in the marketplace, so I use a tequila alternative that is so delicious!

Feeling *Fancy?*
Rub the rim with fresh lime or orange, then dip it in sugar.

1½ ounces NA blanco tequila (I used Trejo's Spirits)

1 ounce cranberry juice

½ ounce lime juice

½ ounce NA triple sec (I used Lyre's Orange Sec)

¼ ounce simple syrup

Ice cubes

Fresh or dehydrated lime or orange slices, for garnishing (page 152)

Place the NA blanco tequila, cranberry and lime juices, triple sec, and simple syrup in a cocktail shaker.

Add some ice and give it a good shake until it's nice and cold.

Strain into a martini glass.

Garnish with some fresh or dehydrated lime or orange slices.

You Put Eggs in That?

Whiskey Sour

Did you know whiskey sours have egg whites in them? I never drank whiskey sours and only ordered cocktails at the bar without knowing what was being poured into them—I was a wine mom through and through. The first time I found out egg whites were an ingredient to this drink, I just couldn't imagine it tasting good, but let me tell you, try it before you deny it. It is delish. 10/10.

2 ounces NA whiskey

1 ounce lemon juice

½ ounce simple syrup

½ ounce egg white (page 20)

Ice cubes

Aromatic or angostura bitters, for garnishing

Lemon slice, for garnishing

Place the NA whiskey, lemon juice, simple syrup, and egg white in a cocktail shaker.

Give it a "dry shake" (shaking without ice) for about 30 seconds, or until frothy.

Add ice and shake until chilled.

Strain into a rocks glass with fresh ice.

Garnish with a few dashes of bitters and a lemon slice.

Conquering the Dark Days

Dark & Stormy

My life felt quite dark and stormy for many years, including, but not limited to, divorce, breast cancer, and the loss of my parents. There were a lot of days that felt like the name of this drink, yet I had never heard of it until I stopped drinking. The irony of learning all about cocktails once I stopped drinking is very much not lost on me. If you're someone who's trying to conquer the dark days, grab a glass and let this mocktail give you the boost to get you through it.

Ice cubes
2 ounces NA dark rum
½ ounce lime juice
Ginger beer
Lime wedge, for garnishing

Add ice to a highball glass (or any glass that makes you happy!).

Pour over the NA dark rum and lime juice.

Top it with your favorite ginger beer (I usually eyeball it until it fills the glass) and stir with a bar spoon.

Garnish with a lime wedge.

Momma's Not Buzzed

Bee's Knees

When I was a camp counselor, my nickname was Buzz. There are some campers who still call me that to this day. But just as that nickname has nothing to do with alcohol, the same goes here. This drink is simple, elevated, and doesn't scream, "Still drinking out of a wine box hidden in the pantry." If you can say, "Momma's not buzzed," and mean it, you can't go wrong.

2 ounces NA gin

1 ounce lemon juice

½ ounce honey syrup

Ice cubes

Lemon twist (page 150), for garnishing

Place the NA gin, lemon juice, and honey syrup in a cocktail shaker. Add some ice.

Shake it up—or shake it off, depending on how your day has been—until chilled.

Strain into a chilled cocktail glass (I love a coupe glass for this one, but you make the rules here).

Garnish with a lemon twist.

Sangria Hacked

Tinto de Verano

*Get ready for the razzle-dazzle. This drink hack was shared with me by Jennifer Page, the first founding member of my **Thriving Alcohol-Free** community. After a long day when I'm feeling decision fatigue, this mocktail has saved me on many occasions when I need to surf the urge but don't want to get out my cocktail shaker. You can also use that yummy soda, Fresca, from the 1970s and '80s—they still make it! Get ready because this might just be your new favorite mocktail, mainly because it is so stupidly easy.*

Alternative!

If you want an aspartame-free option (which I typically do!), substitute the sparkling soda with Zevia Grapefruit Citrus.

Ice cubes

Equal parts grapefruit-flavored sparkling soda (see Alternative!)

Equal parts NA red wine

Add ice to a glass of your choice.

Pour over the sparkling soda and NA red wine and give it a stir.

Don't Be So Old Fashioned

Old-Fashioned

Distracted by wine so much that you've never had an old-fashioned? Get ready to enjoy this nonalcoholic version of a classic cocktail. Far removed from the screw-top wine, this mocktail is sophisticated yet not complicated to make. The best part might just be the giant ice cube, which is used to prevent diluting the drink, unlike smaller ice cubes, crushed ice, or nugget ice, which quickly melts. Bring out the big guns and buy a big, fun ice mold. Let's drink!

Feeling *Fancy?*

If you want to garnish with a twist or spiral, see the Garnish Glossary (page 150).

2½ ounces NA whiskey

½ ounce maple syrup

3 dashes aromatic bitters

1 very large ice cube (recommended, or use smaller ice cubes)

Orange peel, for garnishing

Maraschino cherry, for garnishing

Place the NA whiskey, maple syrup, and aromatic bitters in a rocks glass.

Add one very large ice cube to the glass.

Gently stir with a bar spoon for about 30 seconds, or until the drink is nice and cold.

Add the orange peel to the glass for a garnish, and a maraschino cherry for a classic finish.

Good Ol' G+T

Gin and Tonic

My husband's drink of choice, this NA take is as refreshing as it is easy. It's become a favorite among my friends who have also broken up with their wine habit, for its simplicity and how it helps surf the urge during many a wine witching hour.

Ice cubes

4 lime wheels

2 ounces NA gin

Tonic water

Squeeze of lime juice (optional)

Lime wedge, for garnishing

Add ice to a glass. Tuck lime wheels between the ice cubes and the glass to make it look pretty.

Pour over the NA gin.

Top it with tonic water.

Give a gentle stir with a bar spoon or a stainless-steel straw. If desired, add a squeeze of lime to taste.

Garnish with a lime wedge.

Mocktail Queen

Lemon Drop

You can mocktail / You can thrive / Having the time of your life! *Calling all of my mocktail queens! Or dancing queens if you're new here. It's time to grab some lemons and make yourself a drink that will make you feel like the queen that you are! ABBA, hit it!*

Feeling *Fancy?*

To add an effervescent element, top it with either sparkling water or a nonalcoholic sparkling brut.

2 ounces NA gin

1 ounce lemon juice

1 ounce simple syrup

Ice cubes

Lemon wedge, for the rim

Sugar (or sugar alternative), for the rim

Place the NA gin, lemon juice, and simple syrup in a cocktail shaker.

Add ice and shake until chilled.

Prepare a chilled glass by rubbing the rim with the flesh of a lemon, then dip the rim into sugar, or a sugar alternative, to sweeten every sip. (Or lick the rim; life's a party!)

Strain the mixture into the prepared glass.

Midwest Fizz

Ranch Water

This simple mocktail has only three ingredients: lime juice, NA tequila, and sparkling water. For sparkling water, I highly recommend Topo Chico. If you've never had Topo Chico, as I hadn't (don't judge, I grew up in Philly and now live in Kentucky, not Texas), Topo Chico is a mucho-effervescent sparkling water that will make you want to get up and two-step. Be like the ranchers and make it right in your Topo Chico bottle (see Feeling Fancy?).

Feeling Fancy?

Drink about half of a Topo Chico, then slowly pour in the NA tequila and lime juice.

Lime wedge, for the rim plus 1 for garnishing

Tajín seasoning, for the rim

Ice cubes

2 ounces NA blanco tequila

½ ounce lime juice (or more if you'd like!)

Sparkling water (such as Topo Chico)

Prepare a highball glass by rubbing the rim with the flesh of a lime wedge, then dip the rim in Tajín seasoning.

Add ice to the glass.

Pour over the NA tequila and lime juice.

Top it with sparkling water and give it a stir.

Garnish with a lime wedge.

Not
Past
Our
Prime

Flavor Fiesta
Blackberry Jam Gin

*I love to gather with my favorite ladies for a **Happy Half-Hour** once a week. This drink is always a favorite! With the tangy flavor of blackberry jam, prepare your tastebuds for a flavor fiesta. Gather some friends and throw an impromptu party right in your kitchen.*

1 teaspoon blackberry jam

2 ounces NA gin

¾ ounce lemon juice

½ ounce simple syrup

Ice cubes

Club soda or tonic water

Lemon wedge or fresh or dehydrated lemon slice (page 152), for garnishing

Place the jam, NA gin, lemon juice, and simple syrup in a cocktail shaker.

Add ice and shake until chilled.

Double strain into a highball glass with fresh ice.

Top it with club soda or tonic water.

Garnish with a lemon wedge or a fresh or dehydrated lemon slice.

Time Flies

Maid in Scotland

Remember high school—it was yesterday, right?
Time flies no matter what you do, so I made this
mocktail to celebrate savoring the everyday
moments of life. With the perfect balance of fresh
and hearty flavors, this NA take on a Maid in
Scotland is set to make you remember every sip.

2 or 3 cucumber slices, plus 1 for garnishing

2 or 3 mint leaves, plus 1 for garnishing

¾ ounce lime juice

2 ounces NA whiskey

½ ounce simple syrup

Ice cubes

Muddle the cucumber, mint leaves, and lime juice in a cocktail shaker. Be gentle and don't over muddle your mint friends.

Add the NA whiskey, simple syrup, and ice. Shake until well combined.

Strain into your favorite mocktail glass with fresh ice.

Garnish with a cucumber slice and mint leaf.

When Life Gives You Don Lemon, Make a Mocktail

Lemon Water

Once upon a time, there was a CNN anchor (who will remain nameless). Live on TV, he announced that women in their fifties were "past their prime." What a joke! That comment played on repeat in my head. I'm over fifty and feel like my life is just getting started. My prime time feels like it has finally arrived, and I know many other women feel the same. I dedicate this drink to all the women who, after going through hard times, when life gives them lemons, choose to make the best of things.

Ice cubes

4 ounces coconut water

1 ounce lemon juice

Splash of agave nectar

Sparkling water

Lemon wheel or wedge, for garnishing

To a glass with ice, add the coconut water, lemon juice, and agave. Gently stir.

Top it with sparkling water.

Garnish with a lemon wheel or wedge and enjoy!

Bluegrass Spirit

Kentucky Buck

Step into the heartland of flavor and raise a glass to the spirit of the Bluegrass State. Every sip of this mocktail tells a tale of tradition and the undeniable charm of Kentucky. I love the great state of Kentucky, and I feel so blessed to be living in such a beautiful state with wonderful people. And yes, if you're wondering, most of us have teeth and aren't married to our cousins.

2 or 3 fresh strawberries, hulled, plus 1 for garnishing

½ ounce lemon juice

1½ ounces NA whiskey

½ ounce simple syrup

2 dashes NA aromatic bitters

Ice cubes

Ginger beer

Lemon wheel, for garnishing

Muddle the strawberries in your cocktail shaker.

Add the lemon juice, NA whiskey, simple syrup, and aromatic bitters.

Add ice and shake it up!

Double strain into a glass with fresh ice.

Top it with ginger beer.

Garnish with a lemon wheel and strawberry and enjoy!

Pantry Harmony

Pisco Sour

Try out this hydrating alcohol-free spin of the national drink of Peru, Pisco Sour. Using everyday ingredients found in your pantry, this taste of culture is mighty delish. Including coconut water, you're sure to receive a hydrating shower of goodness upon your every cell.

Feeling Fancy?

Add a few drops of aromatic or angostura bitters on top of the foam to elevate this drink.

3 ounces coconut water

¾ ounce simple syrup

½ ounce lime juice

1 egg white (page 20)

Ice cubes

Fresh or dehydrated lime wheel (page 152), for garnishing

Place the coconut water, simple syrup, lime juice, and egg white in a cocktail shaker. Shake until well combined and frothy.

Add ice and give it another good shake.

Double strain into a chilled coupe glass.

Garnish with a fresh or dehydrated lime wheel.

Berry Basil Bliss

Blueberry Basil

Sing it with me, "Perfection in 1, 2, 3, 4!"
This recipe is so simple and delicious,
and I hope you love it as much as I do!

Top Tip!

If blueberries aren't in season, substitute with frozen blueberries. Simply defrost before muddling. Or try using a different berry!

Handful of blueberries (about 10)

½ ounce simple syrup

4 basil leaves, plus 1 for garnishing

½ ounce lemon juice

1¼ ounces NA gin (such as Amethyst Blueberry Ginger Mint)

Ice cubes

Sparkling water (bonus if lemon-flavored)

Lemon wheel, for garnishing

Muddle-like-a-mother the blueberries and simple syrup in your cocktail shaker.

Add the basil leaves and gently muddle, to release the oils.

Add the lemon juice, NA gin, and ice. Shake it all up.

Strain into a glass filled with fresh ice.

Top it with sparkling water.

Garnish with a lemon wheel or a basil leaf.

You're Special. No, Really.

Mai Tai

Have you tried orgeat? Orgeat is a sweet syrup with a distinct flavor, often associated with almonds. Imagine the taste of a liquid marzipan. Orgeat brings this mocktail a nutty sweetness—kind of like me: sweet, but nuts! If you're like me, you're special. No, really! Don't let anyone tell you that you don't deserve this drink.

2 ounces NA rum
½ ounce orgeat syrup
1½ ounces lime juice
1½ ounces pineapple juice
1 ounce orange juice
Ice cubes
Mint leaf, for garnishing
Lime wedge, for garnishing

Place the NA rum and orgeat syrup in a cocktail shaker with the lime, pineapple, and orange juices.

Add ice, and shake it up, baby!

Strain into a glass with fresh ice.

Make it pretty with a mint leaf and lime wedge garnish.

Seasons of Life

Cinnamon Chai Whiskey

I have to give myself a high-five for making this delicious mocktail. It's always a crowd pleaser. Every sip evokes the essence of the fall season. Who wouldn't want that on their taste buds? Serve this to your friends when toasting to a new season of life.

2½ ounces NA cinnamon whiskey (such as Spiced KY 74 or Beckett's)

1 ounce lemon juice

3 dashes orange bitters

1 ounce chai concentrate (such as Trader Joe's)

Ice cubes

Dehydrated orange slices or orange peel (page 152), for garnishing

Cinnamon stick, for garnishing

Place the NA cinnamon whiskey, lemon juice, orange bitters, and chai concentrate in a mixing glass.

Add ice and stir with a bar spoon.

Place a large ice cube, or a bunch of ice, in a whiskey glass.

Use a Hawthorne strainer to strain the drink into the glass.

Garnish with dehydrated orange slices or an orange peel, and a cinnamon stick.

Spicy Momma Mocktails

Opposites Attract
Spicy Pepino Mocktail

Cucumber has cooling properties, but the jalapeño brings some heat. Opposites attract in this one! If you're in a relationship, you can probably attest to the fact that opposites indeed attract. My husband and I could not be any more different, yet we work great—not perfectly, because there's no such thing (unless you're a mocktail, of course). Enjoy this mocktail with some chips and queso, and dinner is served!

Feeling Extra *Spicy?*
Prepare the glass by rubbing the rim with the flesh of a cucumber, then dip it in Tajín seasoning.

1 or 2 cucumber slices, plus 1 for garnishing

1 or 2 jalapeño slices (or a bar spoonful of jalapeño brine), plus 1 for garnishing

¾ ounce lime juice

2 ounces NA blanco tequila

3 dashes orange bitters

½ ounce agave nectar

½ ounce pineapple juice

Ice cubes

Sparkling water (optional)

In a cocktail shaker, muddle the cucumber, jalapeño slices, and lime juice. Take out all of your aggression; don't worry about being gentle.

Add the NA blanco tequila, orange bitters, agave, and pineapple juice.

Add ice and shake it up until chilled.

Strain into a glass with fresh ice.

If desired, top it with a splash of sparkling water.

Garnish with a cucumber slice and jalapeño slice.

Climb the Mountain

Spicy Strawberry Margarita

Strong women are like GPS systems with a hint of sass. No matter how many detours life throws at us, we always recalibrate and come back with a, "You thought you were going to stop me?" attitude. This drink is in honor of my daughter, Hannah, who overcame enormous obstacles early in life and by God's grace is thriving today in early adulthood. This is a representation of all types of strong women out there who have kept calm and carried on.

Feeling Extra *Spicy?*

Prepare the glass by rubbing the rim with the flesh of a lime, then dip it in Tajín seasoning.

3 to 5 strawberries

1 ounce lime juice

¼ ounce jalapeño brine (or a few muddled jalapeños)

Ice cubes

2 ounces NA tequila

½ ounce agave nectar

Sparkling water (bonus if strawberry-flavored)

Lime wedge, or strawberry or jalapeño slice, for garnishing (optional)

Muddle the strawberries with the lime juice and jalapeño brine in a cocktail shaker.

Add ice, NA tequila, and agave. Shake it up until chilled.

Strain into a glass with fresh ice.

Top it with sparkling water.

If desired, garnish with a lime wedge, or strawberry or jalapeño slice.

Blushing Peaches
Rebel Mocktail

Picture this: Peaches sunbathing in honey at a spicy little fiesta. Buckle up because this is not your average mocktail. This drink is the life of the party, the rebel of the orchard, the reason that peaches blush. It is here to prove that peaches and spice make everything nice.

1 ripe peach, cut into chunks

1 ounce lime juice, plus extra for the rim

½ ounce hot honey (such as Trader Joe's)

2 ounces NA tequila

Ice cubes

Tajín seasoning, for the rim

Peach slice, for garnishing (optional)

Place the chopped peach and lime juice in a cocktail shaker and muddle-like-a-mother!

Add the hot honey, NA tequila, and ice.

Prepare the glass by rubbing the rim with lime juice, then dip the rim in Tajín seasoning.

Strain into a glass with fresh ice.

If desired, garnish with a peach slice.

Fussy Mommy

Spicy Margarita

Save the day with this drink! I love the simplicity and the spice and bite from the jalapeños. Making this drink also uses the method of a Shake and Dump, which means fewer dishes to wash afterwards. No fuss, no muss, which we moms love!

3 or 4 jalapeño slices (or a teaspoon of jalapeño brine), plus more for garnishing

2 ounces NA tequila

1 ounce triple sec

1 ounce lime juice

½ ounce agave nectar

Ice cubes

Lime wheel, for the rim and garnishing

Tajín seasoning, for the rim

Muddle the jalapeños (make sure to remove the seeds), or mash them up directly in a cocktail shaker. Do not worry about over-muddling. The jalapeños can handle taking on your frustrations of the day, so muddle-like-a-mother!

Add the NA tequila, triple sec, lime juice, agave, and ice.

Shake it up until chilled.

Prepare the glass by rubbing the rim with the flesh of a lime, then dip the rim into Tajín seasoning.

Dirty-dump the mixture into the glass. This means pouring without straining—ice and all (it has nothing to do with diapers).

Garnish with a lime wheel or jalapeño slices.

Smoky Mango Mountain

Fiery Mocktail

My Lily named this drink after a wonderful fall break vacation we had in the Smoky Mountains of Tennessee. Where sweetness meets a kick that's sassier than your morning alarm, I'd like to preface this mocktail by saying, "Taste buds, hold on tight. We are about to embark on a flavor rollercoaster and spicy mango is going to be our captain today."

2 ounces mango nectar

¼ ounce orange juice

½ ounce hot honey
    (I used Trader Joe's)

½ ounce lime juice

Ice cubes

Lime wedges, for the rim
    and garnishing

Tajín seasoning, for the rim

Sparkling water (optional)

In a cocktail shaker, add the mango nectar, orange juice, hot honey, and lime juice.

Add the ice and shake it up until chilled.

Prepare a glass by rubbing the rim with the flesh of a lime, then dip the rim in Tajín seasoning.

Strain into a glass with fresh ice.

Garnish with a lime wedge. If you'd like, add a splash of sparkling water.

Hot Flash *Mommas* Need Frozen Drinks

Flashy Frosé

Frozen Strawberry Mocktail

Strip down or throw off the covers and enjoy this frozen mocktail. If you're too young for hot flashes (or your own "personal summer" as my Aunt Kathy calls it), save this entire chapter for summer fun! Meanwhile, the rest of us Gen X-ers will be enjoying these frozen concoctions all year long.

¼ cup ice cubes

4 ounces NA rosé (I used Giesen 0% Rosé)

½ cup (75 g) frozen strawberries

½ ounce simple syrup

Fresh strawberries, for garnishing

Place the ice, NA rosé, strawberries, and simple syrup in a high-powered blender and process until smooth. If the mixture is too thick, add a splash more rosé. If it's too thin, add more ice.

Pour the mixture into a glass.

Garnish with fresh strawberries.

Summertime Refresh

Frozen Watermelon Margarita

My younger daughter, Lily, is obsessed with watermelon. She could eat an entire watermelon every day, and she loves mocktails. We made this incredible frozen watermelon mocktail together. I wish you could have seen her face when she tried it the first time. To quote her: "MOOOOOOOOOOOOM!!! This is SOOOOO GOOD!" I love that my daughter and I can make drinks together, and that I never have to be afraid of her sipping something I am drinking. My drinks are kid-friendly but crafted for an adult palate.

Feeling Fancy?
Prepare the glass by rubbing the rim with the flesh of a lime or watermelon, then dip it into sugar.

1 cup (150 g) frozen watermelon chunks

2 ounces NA tequila, plus more if needed

1 ounce lime juice

½ ounce simple syrup

Water (optional)

Watermelon slice, for garnishing

Lime wheel, for garnishing

Place the watermelon chunks, NA tequila, lime juice, and simple syrup in a high-powered blender and process until smooth. Add another splash of tequila or water if the drink is too thick.

Pour into a mason jar or margarita glass.

Garnish with a watermelon slice and lime wheel.

Chilly Escape

Slushy Coconut Margarita

Adulting can be hard, but choosing which mocktail to drink shouldn't be. Choose this one to freeze the brain of all responsibilities. Life is too short to only focus on ticking off the next thing on the to-do list. Every once in a while, we deserve a chilly escape from the daily grind. Make today that day!

1 cup ice cubes

2½ ounces NA tequila

1 ounce NA triple sec

1 ounce lime juice

1 ounce agave nectar

2 ounces canned coconut milk

Lime wedge, for the rim

Toasted coconut flakes, for the rim

Place the ice, NA tequila, triple sec, lime juice, agave, and coconut milk in a high-powered blender and process until smooth. If the consistency is too thick, add a bit more coconut milk.

Prepare the glass by rubbing the rim with the flesh of a lime, then dip the rim in toasted coconut flakes.

Pour the mixture into the glass and enjoy!

Arctic Orchard Bliss
Frozen Apple Mocktail

This delightful concoction will transport you to a snow-covered orchard where the crispness of the air meets the sweetness of perfectly ripe apples. While this is a frozen apple drink for the summertime, you can drink it whenever you need something ice-cold.

Apple cider

2 ounces NA vodka (see Top Tip!)

¼ ounce honey

Splash of lemon juice

Cinnamon sugar, for the rim

Apple slice or cinnamon stick, for garnishing

In advance, prepare your apple cider ice cubes by pouring apple cider into an ice tray and freezing overnight.

Place the NA vodka, 6 apple cider ice cubes, honey, and lemon juice in a high-powered blender and process until smooth.

Prepare the glass by rubbing the rim with water or apple cider, then dip the rim in cinnamon sugar.

Pour the mixture into the glass.

Garnish with an apple slice or cinnamon stick.

Vacation Mode Loading...

Pina Colada

This is not just a mocktail, this is your express ticket to a sweet-treat mental vacation, where deadlines are distant memories and palm trees are your personal assistants. Grab your shades and start collecting those tiny umbrellas. Vacation Mode Loading ... is ready to transport you to a blissful state where the only thing loading is your mocktail. Cheers to the smell of salty air and seashells in the sand.

1 cup ice cubes

4 ounces pineapple juice

2 ounces coconut cream

Maraschino cherry, for garnishing (optional)

Place the ice, pineapple juice, and coconut cream in a high-powered blender and process until smooth.

Pour the mixture into a glass.

Garnish with a cherry, and a mini umbrella, if you're feeling fancy. Bon voyage!

Mammy Graham Mocktail

Strawberry Slush

At the age of forty-four, after a routine mammogram, I was asked to come back for a biopsy. That biopsy turned into two, which ended up being breast cancer. Here's my tip to you—get your girls checked. Mark it on the calendar. Make the appointment. Just do it. I am grateful for that routine mammogram that detected my breast cancer early. Give yourself a little reward afterwards, such as this mocktail.

¾ cup (110 g) frozen strawberries, plus more for garnishing

1 cup cold coconut milk

1 ounce honey

Maple syrup or honey, for the rim

Graham crackers, finely crushed, for the rim

Whipped cream, for garnishing

Place the strawberries, coconut milk, and honey in a high-powered blender and process until smooth.

Prepare the glass by coating the rim with maple syrup or honey, then dip the rim in finely crushed graham crackers.

Pour the mixture into the glass.

Garnish with whipped cream and strawberries.

Buzzworthy
Brunch
Minus
the
Buzz

Lily's Lavender Royale

French 75

My Lily LOVES lavender. L.O.V.E. Love. She's obsessed. This lavender drink takes on the classic French 75. I dedicate it to my sweet girl who is growing up way too fast.

Ice cubes

1½ ounces NA gin

¾ ounce lemon juice

½ ounce lavender syrup

2 dashes lavender bitters (optional)

NA sparkling white wine (or No-Secco, sparkling brut, or Classico)

Lemon slice or dried lavender buds, for garnishing

In a cocktail shaker with ice, add the NA gin, lemon juice, lavender syrup, and lavender bitters, if using.

Shake it up until chilled and strain into a coupe glass.

Top it with NA sparkling white wine.

Garnish with a lemon slice or lavender buds.

Wellness Retreat

Ginger Mimosa

Imagine your mimosa went on a wellness retreat where it received a ginger-infused pep talk. With this drink, we welcome back the new and refreshed product. Mothers everywhere deserve to go on a wellness retreat at some point in their life, but let's be real, just having time alone in the car or on a trip to the store can be as refreshing as a full-blown wellness retreat. Start small with this mocktail.

Ice cubes

2 ounces sparkling NA white wine

2 ounces orange juice

3 ounces ginger beer

½ ounce lime juice

Dehydrated orange slice (page 152), for garnishing

Add ice to a mason jar.

Pour the NA white wine, orange juice, ginger beer, and lime juice over the ice.

Garnish with a dehydrated orange slice.

Love Dove

Paloma

Did you know the Paloma, not the margarita, is the national cocktail of Mexico? (Paloma also means "dove" in Spanish—just so you're prepared for the next episode of Jeopardy. You're welcome.) This drink is super easy to prepare, but if you don't have NA tequila simply eliminate the ingredient. Keep calm and move on.

Top Tip!

To make this mocktail even simpler, substitute the grapefruit juice, agave, and sparkling water with grapefruit soda.

2 ounces NA tequila

2 ounces grapefruit juice, plus extra for the rim

½ ounce lime juice, plus extra for the rim

½ ounce agave nectar

Ice cubes

Salt, for the rim

Sparkling water

Rosemary sprig, for garnishing

In a cocktail shaker, add the NA tequila, grapefruit and lime juices, and agave.

Add ice and shake until chilled.

Prepare the glass by dipping the rim in lime or grapefruit juice, then dip the rim in salt.

Strain the mixture into the prepared glass with or without ice. Top it with sparkling water.

Garnish with rosemary.

Easy Like Monday Morning

Blood Orange Mocktail

It's time to look forward to Monday mornings the same way we do Sunday mornings. There is something about looking forward to a reward on what could be considered a tough day that makes it that much more doable. Add this drink to your morning routine and let it tell Monday who's in charge. With this boost, you'll be moving through the day feeling lighter than normal.

1¼ ounces blood orange juice

2 ounces NA whiskey

½ ounce simple syrup

1 ounce lemon juice

Ice cubes

Lime sparkling water

Place the blood orange juice, NA whiskey, simple syrup, and lemon juice in a cocktail shaker and shake it up.

Strain into a glass with ice.

Top it with lime sparkling water for a delicious fizzy drink.

Aperol Sunshine
Euro-Margarita

Who says margaritas can't have a little European flair? A spritz of sophistication? This cross-cultural mocktail is a fusion of global flavors that will transport your taste buds to new adventures if you maybe haven't been on many transcontinental vacations recently (my passport has definitely been neglected!). Maybe it'll inspire your next great adventure, too.

Ice cubes

½ ounce NA Aperol

1 ounce NA blanco tequila

½ ounce lime juice

½ ounce agave nectar

Sparkling water (plain or orange-flavored)

Orange slice, for garnishing

In a cocktail shaker with ice, add the NA Aperol, blanco tequila, lime juice, and agave. Shake until chilled.

Strain into a glass with fresh ice.

Top it with sparkling water.

Garnish with an orange slice.

Feeling Fancy

Peachberry Bellini

A bubbly drink that makes sparkling water jealous. Grab a fancy flute and put on your sparkliest personality and clothes, then let this drink turn your night into a bubbly bash! Whoever told you that sparkles were out is not invited.

Top Tip!

If you're in a rush and can't make the peachberry puree, add some peach juice to the bottom of the glass instead.

Makes 2 servings

PEACHBERRY PUREE

1 ripe peach

6 strawberries

¼ ounce simple syrup

1 ounce lemon juice

¼ cup water

MOCKTAIL

NA sparkling white wine, chilled (My favorites are Giesen 0% Sparkling Brut or Jøyus)

To make the peachberry puree (or see Top Tip!)

Peel the peach and chop it up. Discard the pit.

Place the peach, strawberries, simple syrup, lemon juice, and water in a high-powered blender and process until smooth. If time permits, store the mixture in the refrigerator for an hour before serving.

To make the mocktail

Place a tablespoon of peachberry puree at the bottom of two flute glasses.

Fill the glass halfway with the chilled NA sparkling wine and stir slightly until the flute's contents are just starting to combine.

After the fizz settles, top off the glasses with more sparkling wine.

Spiced Virgin Mary

Bloody Mary

Drink your vegetables with this mocktail that's packed with nutrients. Tomato juice has lycopene, an excellent antioxidant that loves to kick ass and take no prisoners. One of the best things about a Bloody Mary is the garnishes, so go crazy with this one! You cannot go wrong with this classic.

BLOODY MARY SALT

¼ teaspoon paprika

¼ teaspoon salt

¼ teaspoon garlic powder

¼ teaspoon onion powder

MOCKTAIL

Lemon wedges, for the rim and garnishing

3 ounces tomato juice

¼ ounce lemon juice

1 ounce pickle brine

¼ teaspoon horseradish

Dash Worcestershire sauce

Pinch of cayenne pepper

Dash hot sauce

Celery heart stalk, for garnishing

To make the Bloody Mary salt

Mix the paprika, salt, garlic powder, and onion powder on a plate. I have given you measurements, but as always, modify for your taste buds.

To make the mocktail

Prepare the glass by rubbing the rim with the flesh from a lemon wedge, then dip the rim into the Bloody Mary salt.

Place the tomato and lemon juices, pickle brine, horseradish, Worcestershire sauce, cayenne pepper, and hot sauce in a cocktail shaker.

Shake until well combined.

Strain into the prepared glass while saying, "Ooooooh la la!"

Garnish with a celery stalk and lemon wedge.

Mint
to Be
Mocktails .

Must Be Mint

Mint Julep

Living in Kentucky, a Mint Julep is a must, as it is the official cocktail of the Kentucky Derby. When I say the Derby is bigger here than Christmas, I am not joking. The festivities go on for weeks. People greet you with, "Have a great Derby," and "Happy Derby." If you're planning a business meeting, people may respond with, "Call me after Derby." It may be tricky to keep up with all of the parties and festivals, but Kentucky does it right, so here's the perfect mocktail to enjoy at your Derby.

6 to 8 mint leaves, plus more for garnishing

½ ounce simple syrup

Crushed ice

2½ ounces NA whiskey

Splash of cold water

In a glass, muddle the mint leaves and simple syrup.

Add the crushed ice, NA whiskey, and a splash of cold water and gently stir with a bar spoon.

Garnish with mint leaves and enjoy this perfect taste of Kentucky!

K.I.S.S.

Mojito

If you were worried that there wasn't going to be an NA mojito recipe in this chapter, worry no more! There's just something about a simple, refreshing drink that can be made wherever you are. A classic drink you'll want to add to all of your party menus, I promise you'll never get tired of keeping it stupid simple.

Top Tip!

Make this mocktail even easier by using sparkling lime water, like Spindrift, to substitute the lime juice and sparkling water.

1 ounce lime juice

¾ ounce simple syrup

Several mint leaves

Ice cubes

2 ounces NA white rum (I love Lyre's White Cane Spirit)

Sparkling water

Mint sprigs, for garnishing

Lime wedge, for garnishing

Gently muddle the lime juice, simple syrup, and mint leaves in a glass.

Add the ice and NA white rum and stir until well combined.

Top it with sparkling water.

Garnish with mint sprigs and a lime wedge.

Stuck in a Coconut Tree

Coconut Fizz

Need a vacation in a glass? Make this mocktail in the middle of winter and I guarantee you'll be transported to a tropical island. The coconut flavors give you the fresh taste of the tropics, and if you decide you're feeling fancy, the entire aesthetic is sure to scream, "I'm on vacation."

Feeling Fancy?

Coat the rim in honey or lime juice, then dip it into a mixture of toasted coconut flakes and lime zest.

- 5 to 7 mint leaves, plus more for garnishing
- 1 ounce lime juice (plus more for taste)
- Ice cubes
- 2½ ounces NA rum (such as Beckett's Coconut to add some extra coconut flavor)
- 2 ounces coconut milk, canned (or coconut cream or coconut water)
- ½ ounce simple syrup
- Sparkling water
- Lime wedge, for garnishing

In a glass, gently muddle the mint leaves and lime juice. Don't over-muddle! Be gentle enough to release the oils of the mint.

Fill the glass with ice.

In a cocktail shaker, add the NA rum, coconut milk, simple syrup, and ice and shake it up until chilled.

Strain into the glass.

Top it with sparkling water.

Garnish with a lime wedge and mint leaves.

Taste and See with GaryVee

Blueberry Spritz

This mocktail is in honor of the only man I will allow to curse at me all day long: Gary Vaynerchuck. Gary loves blueberries, but he also inspired me to start my Instagram account, Mocktail Mom, in 2021. I had zero experience making drinks or making videos, but Gary encourages people to try new things; I call it the "taste and see" attitude. Whatever new thing you want to try, give it a go, and see what happens! It could end up changing the trajectory of your life, as making mocktail videos has changed mine. Thanks, Gary.

Handful of blueberries (about 10)

6 mint leaves

½ ounce simple syrup

Ice cubes

2 ounces NA gin

Lemon-lime sparkling water (such as Betty Buzz)

Gently muddle the blueberries, mint, and simple syrup in a glass.

Add ice and pour over the NA gin. Stir with a bar spoon.

Top it with lemon-lime sparkling water.

Havana Dream

Old Cuban

My dad, Herb Links, wanted to visit Cuba more than anything, but he never made it before passing away at eighty. He loved to meet people from Cuba and loved to wear his Guayabera shirts. He would have fit right in had he ever made it to the island. This drink is dedicated to my wonderful dad.

¾ ounce lime juice

Several mint leaves, plus 1 for garnishing

2 ounces dark NA rum

¾ ounce simple syrup

2 dashes aromatic bitters

Ice cubes

NA sparkling brut or dealcoholized sparkling wine

Dehydrated lime (page 152), for garnishing

Gently muddle the lime juice and several mint leaves in a cocktail shaker.

Add the NA rum, simple syrup, aromatic bitters, and ice and shake it all up.

Double strain into a coupe glass. Double straining doesn't take double the effort, it just prevents bits of mint from floating in your drink.

Top it with NA sparkling brut (my favorites are Giesen, Jøyus, and Lyre's Classico).

Garnish with a dehydrated lime and mint leaf.

Mind of Her Own

Gin Mojito

Mint has a mind of its own. It goes wherever it darn well pleases and doesn't apologize. I wasn't a gin drinker before I broke up with alcohol, but I have fallen in love with NA gin—it is just so refreshing and delicious when added to mocktails. Drink this on a hot summer day or for sipping on the patio.

1 lime

Handful of mint leaves (6 to 12)

¾ ounce simple syrup

Ice cubes

2 ounces NA gin (such as Monday)

Sparkling water

Lime wedge, for garnishing

Cut the lime into quarters. Muddle the limes like there is no tomorrow directly in your glass of choice.

Add the mint and simple syrup and gently muddle again (go easy on the mint leaves this time).

Add the ice and the NA gin to the glass. Stir with a bar spoon.

Top it with sparkling water.

Garnish with a lime wedge and mint leaves.

Mules
for
Days

Autumn Orchard

Caramel Apple Mule

I love this one so much, primarily because of the fancy way to rim the glass. It is decadent deliciousness. You'll be so busy eating the caramel that you might forget to make the drink in the end (which I definitely wouldn't know from personal experience)!

Feeling Fancy?

Use spiced whiskey for the NA whiskey. I love Kentucky 74 Spiced or Beckett's Cinnamon Whiskey.

2 caramels, melted, for the rim

Cinnamon sugar, for the rim

Ice cubes

2 ounces NA whiskey (see Feeling Fancy?)

3 ounces ginger beer

3 ounces apple cider

½ ounce lime juice

Apple slice, for garnishing

Cinnamon stick, for garnishing (optional)

Prepare the copper cup by dipping the rim in melted caramel. (Just a few seconds in the microwave will soften the caramel, then let it cool a little before dipping the rim.) Then dip the rim into cinnamon sugar.

Add ice to the prepared cup.

Add the NA whiskey, ginger beer, apple cider, and lime juice and stir until well combined.

Garnish with an apple slice and cinnamon stick (if using).

Jam Session
Jammy Jam Mule

Pick a jam, any jam, that speaks to your taste buds.
It can be peach or whatever you have in your fridge.
You don't have to spend too much on fancy jelly—
well, you can, but it will still be delicious if you don't.

2 ounces NA tequila

1 to 2 tablespoons jam of choice

½ ounce lime juice

Ice cubes

Ginger beer

Lime wedge or fruit, for garnishing

Place the NA tequila, jam, and lime juice in a copper cup and mix until well combined with a spoon.

Add ice and top it with ginger beer.

Garnish with a lime wedge, or fruit that goes with your jam.

Cranberry Dream
Mule 2.0

Move over regular mules, I brought cranberries, and they are here to sleigh! Let your cranberries and ginger beer have a dance off in a copper mug when creating this festive fizz. It is sure to be the life of the party!

Ice cubes

2 ounces NA whiskey

1 ounce cranberry juice

½ ounce lime juice

Ginger beer

Lime wedge or cranberries, for garnishing

In a glass filled with ice, add the NA whiskey, and cranberry and lime juices. Give it a stir.

Top it with ginger beer.

Garnish with a lime wedge or cranberries.

On the Island
Tropical Mule

Escape to a private island of paradise with this mocktail. And by private island, I mean your favorite chair in the living room, since I know we moms can never really take a vacation away from the little ones. With this drink in hand, chillax with the sweet flavors of the tropics that perfectly suit a real private island vacation.

Ice cubes

2 ounces NA coconut rum (I love Beckett's)

½ ounce lime juice

2 ounces pineapple juice

Ginger beer (I love Q Mixers Hibiscus for this recipe)

In a cocktail shaker with ice, add the NA coconut rum, and lime and pineapple juices.

Shake it up until chilled.

Strain into a copper cup with fresh ice.

Top it with ginger beer and gently stir.

Gin-gle Bells Mule
Gin Mule

Enjoy this pretty special drink that surfs the urge with the spirit of gin! This delicious mocktail is a playful twist on the traditional mule. For my gin lovers out there, try this one!

Ice cubes

2 ounces NA gin

½ ounce lime juice

½ ounce simple syrup

Ginger beer

Lime wedge, for garnishing

Fill a copper mug with ice.

Add the NA gin, lime juice, and simple syrup.

Top it with ginger beer until the mug is full.

Garnish with a lime wedge on the rim.

Pumpkin Spice, Everything Nice

Autumn Spice Mule

Come the fall season when things start to get busy—schedules become so hectic, it's hard to keep up—turn to this mocktail. Perfect for entertaining with seasonal flavors or just enjoying a love for pumpkin. Celebrate the return of the pumpkin season again with this mule.

Ice cubes

1 bar spoonful pumpkin puree

¼ teaspoon pumpkin pie spice

2 ounces NA cinnamon whiskey

½ ounce lime juice

Ginger beer

Lime wedge or cinnamon stick, for garnishing

In a cocktail shaker with ice, add the pumpkin puree and pumpkin pie spice and mix with a spoon.

Add the NA cinnamon whiskey and lime juice and give it a good shake!

Strain into a mule cup with fresh ice.

Top it with ginger beer.

Garnish with a lime wedge or cinnamon stick.

Sharing Is Caring

My Lips Taste like Sangria

Red Wine Sangria

Make this recipe for ladies' night, book club, or the average Thursday hang out—or if you're just thirsty. This drink is a free-for-all when it comes to fruit, so feel free to throw in any fruit that you have on hand—anything from slices of apples and oranges or handfuls of berries will work.

Makes 6 to 8 servings

1 bottle NA red wine

½ cup NA whiskey

1½ cups orange juice

¼ cup lemon juice

Several handfuls of fruit of your choice (use apples, oranges, peaches, or berries), plus extra for garnishing

Ice cubes

Sparkling water

In a serving pitcher, mix the NA wine, NA whiskey, and orange and lemon juices.

Add the fruit and stir. Then let sit in the fridge for 30 minutes, or overnight.

Strain into a glass with ice and top it with sparkling water. The glass should be two-thirds mocktail mixture and one-third sparkling water.

Garnish with your choice of fresh fruit.

Shandy Sandy

Shandy

My mom was Sandy, and she was the cream of the crop. Best mother ever. Pearls of wisdom poured from her lips. I don't know how I won the lottery of life to be Sandy Links' daughter, but I am forever thankful! Even if you aren't a beer person, I dare you to try this on a hot summer day and see if you don't fall in love all over again. This recipe is also very carefree; simply mix beer with something yummy and voilà, you've got yourself a shandy!

Top Tip!

If you don't want to use lemonade, substitute it with the juice of several lemons or lemon-lime soda.

Makes 6 to 8 servings

- 3 cups lemonade (see Top Tip!)
- 3 cups NA beer (use a light beer, such as a pale ale, wheat beer, or pilsner)
- Lemon slice, for garnishing

Pour equal parts lemonade and NA beer into a pitcher. If you prefer more of a lemon flavor, add more lemonade. If you prefer more beer flavor, go heavy on the beer.

Garnish with a lemon slice.

Kinda Don't Care

Cider Sangria

This is one of those recipes where you can toss a bunch of ingredients into a pitcher and mix it all together and it'll always come out delicious. If you don't have one or two ingredients, improvise with something else. Make it how you want. I kinda don't care. That's what happens when you're over fifty. It's the best thing ever. (Prime time!)

Makes 6 to 8 servings

½ cup NA whiskey

1 bottle NA white wine

2 cups apple cider

2 apples, sliced, plus more for garnishing

6 cinnamon sticks, plus more for garnishing

Ice cubes

Ginger beer or sparkling water

In a serving pitcher, mix the NA whiskey and white wine, apple cider, apple slices, and cinnamon sticks. Stir to your heart's content.

Set in the fridge for 30 minutes, or until your company arrives.

Pour the mixture into a glass with ice, leaving room to top it with ginger beer or sparkling water.

Garnish with apple slices and a cinnamon stick.

Drinks Well with Friends

Mimosa

Just because you aren't drinking, doesn't mean you can't have a mimosa. Use some nice NA sparkling white wine or prosecco and your friends will probably never know it's a mocktail.

Makes 6 servings

1 bottle of NA sparkling white wine
2½ cups fresh-squeezed orange juice

Make sure your ingredients have had time to chill in the refrigerator beforehand.

Pour the NA white wine and orange juice into a serving pitcher. Give it a gentle stir.

Serve in fancy flute glasses.

My Old Kentucky Home
Porch Punch Sangria

In 2010, I moved from the California seaside to Goshen, Kentucky. I will never get over how kind our neighbors were. But I will also never forget hearing over one hundred thousand people sing "My Old Kentucky Home" before the Kentucky Derby at Churchill Downs. What an emotional moment. I am grateful for the fine people of Kentucky and this wonderful place I get to raise my daughters. I might be a transplant, but Kentucky has my heart.

Makes 6 to 8 servings

Ice cubes

12 ounces NA whiskey

1 bottle NA red wine

1 orange, lemon, and lime, sliced, plus more slices for garnishing

1½ cups (375 g) frozen peaches, sliced

1 liter bottle sparkling lemon-lime soda

In a punch bowl with ice, add the NA whiskey, NA red wine, and orange, lemon, lime, and peach slices. Stir together.

Gently pour in the sparkling lemon-lime soda.

Serve over fresh ice and garnish with a slice of fresh fruit.

Holidays
without
Hangovers.

Comfort Coffee

Irish Coffee

When I'm not going through hot flashes, this delish hot drink makes the perfect treat for cold nights. However, I recommend using decaf coffee if you're making it in the evenings, or else you'll be jeopardizing a good night's sleep.

6 ounces freshly brewed black coffee

1 teaspoon brown sugar

1 ounce NA whiskey alternative

Heavy cream, lightly whipped

Fill a glass with freshly brewed coffee.

Add the brown sugar and stir until dissolved.

Stir in the NA whiskey alternative.

Top with whipped cream.

Let's Stay Home

Hot Toddy

I think most women my age love to stay home. Don't get me wrong, we love to travel and go out to see friends, but come 8pm, we want to be in our robes at home. Even if you're not a homebody, drink this on a cold night. Or when you don't feel well and need to soothe a sore throat. This is my winter favorite drink, perfect for sipping by the fire.

2 ounces NA whiskey
4 ounces hot water
1 tablespoon honey
½ ounce lemon juice

Place the NA whiskey, hot water, honey, and lemon juice in a mug.

Gently mix and enjoy!

Shamrock Shine

Matcha Mocktail

Matcha is a known antioxidant and fantastic for boosting energy. With its natural green hue, add in some green limes for extra color and flavor, and you're all set for a happy St. Paddy's Day.

Feeling *Fancy?*

To make it extra green and boost the flavor, tuck extra lime wheels around the sides and between the ice.

1 teaspoon matcha green tea powder

¾ cup warm water

¼ ounce maple syrup

4 mint leaves, plus 1 for garnishing

½ ounce lime juice

Ice cubes

Tonic water

Lime wheel, for garnishing

In a small bowl, mix the matcha and warm water until the powder is dissolved. Add the maple syrup and stir.

In a glass, muddle the mint leaves and lime juice.

Fill the glass with ice and add the matcha mixture.

Top it with tonic water and stir.

Garnish with a mint leaf and lime wheel.

Harvest Spice Delight

Pumpkin Pie Mocktini

The drink that proves pumpkins aren't meant just for pies. Sip on this mocktail during the autumn season for all those fall vibes!

1 heaping tablespoon pumpkin puree

¼ teaspoon pumpkin pie spice, plus more for garnishing

½ ounce maple syrup

2½ ounces cold milk of choice

2 caramels, melted, for the rim

Cinnamon sugar, for the rim

Whipped cream, for garnishing

In a cocktail shaker, add the pumpkin puree, pumpkin pie spice, maple syrup, and milk. Shake until well combined.

Prepare the glass by dipping the rim in melted caramel, then dip the coated rim in cinnamon sugar.

Pour the mixture into the prepared glass.

Top it with a dollop of whipped cream and an extra sprinkle of pumpkin pie spice.

Wicked Queen's Mocktail

Poison Apple

A wickedly delightful mocktail *cue mischievous giggle into glass*. Even Snow White would be tempted to try this intriguing potion. Make this for spooky season, themed parties, or just for fun. I always opt for fun.

Ice cubes

2½ ounces NA apple vodka (I used Clean Co.)

2 ounces apple cider

1 ounce lemon juice

½ ounce simple syrup

¼ ounce (or a splash) tart cherry juice

Lemon wedge, for the rim

Cinnamon sugar, for the rim

Apple slice, for garnishing

To a cocktail shaker with ice, add the NA apple vodka, apple cider, lemon juice, simple syrup, and cherry juice and shake it up!

Prepare a mason jar by rubbing the rim with the flesh of a lemon, then dip the rim in a cinnamon sugar mixture.

Dirty-dump the mixture, including the ice, into the mason jar. Add additional ice if necessary.

Garnish with an apple slice.

December to Remember

Candy Cane Mocktini

It's not the car in the driveway with a big red bow, but this drink will help you celebrate the holidays and not walk away with fuzzy memories. You'll remember it all—the good, the bad, and the ugly. No matter how your holidays go, this mocktail is sure to be part of the good!

½ ounce sweetened chocolate syrup, for the rim

2 mini candy canes, 1 finely crushed for the rim and 1 for garnishing

Ice cubes

3 ounces cream soda

2 drops peppermint extract

1½ ounces half-and-half

Prepare the martini glass by dipping the rim in chocolate syrup, then dip the rim in finely crushed candy cane.

Place the glass in the freezer for a few minutes while you make the mocktail.

In a mixing glass with ice, add the cream soda, peppermint extract, and half-and-half and stir.

Strain the mixture into the prepared glass.

Garnish with a mini candy cane.

Cranberry Wonderland

Cranberry Whiskey

Big Time Cheers to all things cranberry from Thanksgiving to New Year's! This combination works so well during the winter months. Now's your chance to add it to the menu at your next festive feast.

Ice cubes

2 ounces NA whiskey

2 ounces cranberry juice

2 ounces orange juice

Sparkling water

Cranberries and rosemary sprig, for garnishing

Place the ice, NA whiskey, and cranberry and orange juices in a cocktail shaker.

Shake it up until chilled.

Strain the mixture into the glass.

Top it with sparkling water.

Garnish with cranberries and a rosemary sprig.

Garnish Glossary

Garnishes are like the final frontier of a mocktail, or in other words, the cherry on top. These fabulous little touches can be just for show (a pineapple frond or drink umbrella), for visual and aromatic appeal (a rosemary sprig), or meant to be eaten (a cherry). While the garnishes in my recipes are considered optional, coming from someone who is the laziest garnisher ever, if I can do it, so can you!

Here are some you can simply add to your drinks with no fuss:

- Candied fruit
- Cinnamon stick
- Decorative picks
- Drink stirrers
- Drink umbrellas
- Edible flowers
- Fruit slices or wedges
- Maraschino cherry
- Mini clothespins
- Pineapple fronds
- Vegetables

The following are a few fun hacks that will immediately elevate your drinks and impress your guests.

Citrus twists or spirals: Simply twist a slice of orange peel with your fingers over the mocktail, then drop the peel into the drink. You can also tightly wrap it around a straw to create a coil; gently wrap a spiral strip around a garnish pick or skewer; or tie your zest strip into a little knot. Have fun with it!

HOW TO MAKE A CITRUS SPIRAL

Option 1: Use a sharp knife to cut a thin slice of your citrus fruit. Then make a small cut on one side and cut the peel away from the sweet meat.

Option 2: Use a channel knife, specifically designed for making citrus spirals. Hold the citrus fruit firmly in one hand. Press the channel knife into the fruit's skin near the top, then carefully slide it down along the surface to create a long, spiraling strip of zest.

Dehydrated fruit slices: I wish I had been using dehydrated fruit when I first started drinking mocktails. I make these in my oven, but you can also order them online. They keep for a long time, and they add aromatics and visual appeal.

BRING THE SPARKLE!

Remember, garnishes add a sparkle, flavor, and enhance the whole experience of your mocktail. Get creative while making your drinks pretty. As long as you have fun, anything can be considered a garnish.

DEHYDRATING FRUIT SLICES

Making these takes some time and patience, but it is doable and makes your house smell like a citrus grove!

1. Set the oven to 170°F (76°C) or the lowest setting possible.

2. Wash your fruit and pat dry with paper towel.

3. Thinly slice the fruit. Try to cut the slices to the same thickness so they dehydrate at the same speed. (Use a mandolin if you have one, but a sharp knife will do.)

4. Line a baking sheet with parchment paper. Place a single layer of citrus slices on the prepared sheet. Bake in the oven for approximately 1 hour. Flip the slices and bake for about another hour. Keep an eye on them and make sure they don't turn dark brown. Depending on how thick your slices are some fruits may take more time than others to dry out.

5. Take the fruit out of the oven when it looks brittle, or when a paper towel pressed to the fruit comes away dry.

6. Allow the fruit to cool completely either on a drying rack or on the baking sheet.

7. Store in a sealed container. If the fruit is sufficiently dried out, these garnishes can last on the shelf for about a year.

Herbs: Fresh herbs can be a powerhouse when it comes to crafting a mocktail. Not only do they add instant aromatics, but also you can grab them straight from your garden if you have one. My favorites are basil, mint, thyme, and rosemary.

KEEPING YOUR HERBS ALIVE

For soft herbs, like basil and mint:

1. Wash and dry.

2. Trim the ends of the stems.

3. Fill a glass with an inch of water and add the herbs like a baby bouquet.

4. Leave the basil uncovered and at room temperature. For the mint, loosely cover the bouquet with a plastic bag and store in the refrigerator.

5. Change the water as needed, or when it is no longer clear.

For woodier herbs, like thyme, rosemary, and sage:

1. Wash and dry.

2. Lay in a single layer on a damp paper towel.

3. Gently roll up the paper towel and place in a plastic bag.

4. Store in the refrigerator.

When Dining Out

- Look at the menu ahead of time for nonalcoholic options or one-spirit cocktails that could be easily modified.
- Talk to your server or bartender and ensure they understand that you are ordering a nonalcoholic drink, not a low-alcohol drink.
- Watch the bartender making the drink.
- Have a friend taste it first if you're still wary.

If none of the previous tips work out, come prepared with your own recipe. Here's a few to get you started:

Spicy Pineapple: Muddle jalapeños and pineapple (or jalapeño and pineapple juice), add ice, and top it with club soda.

Seven Bull: Equal parts Red Bull, equal parts lemon-lime soda.

Cranberry Fizz: Club soda and a splash of cranberry in a rocks glass. Garnish with a lime.

Highball Mocktail: Ginger beer, 4 dashes of orange bitters, and a squeeze of a lime, in a highball glass. (Shout-out to Richard Loud, who shared this recipe with me on Episode 9 of my podcast, **Thriving Alcohol-Free**.)

Grapefruit Pom: Club soda, grapefruit juice, and a splash of grenadine.

Lemon Bitter: Club soda, a few dashes of bitters, and a splash of lemon juice.

Bloody Mary: Order it without the vodka; you'll never know the difference.

Liquid Measurement Conversion Table

½ fl oz	1 tablespoon	15 ml
¾ fl oz	1½ tablespoons	22 ml
1 fl oz	2 tablespoons	30 ml
2 fl oz	¼ cup	60 ml
3 fl oz	6 tablespoons	90 ml
4 fl oz	½ cup	120 ml
5 fl oz	10 tablespoons	150 ml
6 fl oz	¾ cup	180 ml
8 fl oz	1 cup	240 ml
16 fl oz	2 cups / 1 pint	475 ml

Acknowledgments

Without God's grace upon grace nothing in my life would be possible. Thank you, Lord, for your mercy and forgiveness.

Since I was five years old, I wanted to be a mom—not necessarily Mocktail Mom, just a mom. Hannah and Lily, you are the greatest joys of my life and I love being your mom. Thank you for supporting me on my crazy mocktail journey.

To my Larry, thank you for helping with so many things, like showing up after work with two beverage refrigerators to help corral my nonalcoholic habit. Your love and care are an incredible gift, and I am thankful you waited forty-five years for me. I love you so much!

This book would not be here if it weren't for the encouraging words I hear in my mind of my parents affirming their belief in me and my capabilities.

To my sisters and the friends that are like sisters—I am so grateful for your love, support, and encouragement!

A special thanks to the women in my membership, **Thriving Alcohol-Free**, and so many in the online sober community that cheer me on and have made my alcohol-free lifestyle so much fun!

Index

© 2024 by Quarto Publishing Group USA Inc.
Text © 2024 by Mocktail Mom™

First published in 2024 by Rock Point,
an imprint of The Quarto Group,
142 West 36th Street, 4th Floor,
New York, NY 10018, USA
(212) 779-4972 www.Quarto.com

Rock Point titles are also available at discount for
retail, wholesale, promotional, and bulk purchase.
For details, contact the Special Sales Manager by
email at specialsales@quarto.com or by mail at
The Quarto Group, Attn: Special Sales
Manager, 100 Cummings Center Suite 265D,
Beverly, MA 01915 USA.

10 9 8 7 6 5 4 3 2 1

ISBN: 978-1-57715-437-2

Digital edition published in 2024
eISBN: 978-0-76038-984-3

Library of Congress Cataloging-in-Publication Data

Names: Podlogar, Debbie, author.
Title: The happiest hour : delicious mocktails for a
    fabulous moms' night in / Debbie Podlogar.
Description: New York, NY, USA : Rock Point,
    2024. | Includes index. |Summary: "The
    Happiest Hour is a delicious collection of over
    50 alcohol-free cocktail recipes so all the
    mothers out there can have fun with mocktails"--
    Provided by publisher.
Identifiers: LCCN 2024006073 (print) | LCCN
    2024006074 (ebook) | ISBN 9781577154372
    (hardcover) | ISBN 9780760389843 (ebook)
Subjects: LCSH: Non-alcoholic beverages.
    | Cocktails. | LCGFT: Cookbooks.
Classification: LCC TX815 .P63 2024 (print) | LCC
    TX815 (ebook) | DDC 641.2/6--dc23
    eng/20240214
LC record available at https://lccn.loc
    gov/2024006073
LC ebook record available at https://lccn.loc
    gov/2024006074

Group Publisher: Rage Kindelsperger
Editorial Director: Erin Canning
Creative Director: Laura Drew
Senior Art Director: Marisa Kwek
Managing Editor: Cara Donaldson
Editor: Katelynn Abraham
Cover Design: Marisa Kwek
Interior Design: Maeve Bargman
Photographer and Food Stylist: Jen Straus

Printed in China